MAY

Ellen Jackson

Illustrated by
Kay Life

Charlesbridge

To Juliana McIntyre, with thanks
—E. J.

With love to my furry,
floppy-eared friend, Kimberley
—K. L.

Did You Know?

May is a month of outdoor fun. The ice and snow of winter have melted, but the heat of summer has not begun.

In May, nature is throbbing with life. A chorus of birds sings in the morning, and bees hum beneath the sky. Flowers bloom everywhere—in gardens, in the deserts, and on the prairies. White, pink, and gold petals from blossoming trees spill across city lawns.

As spring moves toward summer, many animals are busy with their young. Mosquitoes and black flies lay their eggs in ponds and lakes. Mother raccoons search for fruits, vegetables, seeds, and birds' eggs to feed their babies. Female deer, called does, stand watch over new fawns that lie hidden among leaves on the forest floor.

People, too, are outside enjoying the mild May weather. Children zip down sidewalks on bikes, Rollerblades, and skateboards.

The air rings with the thwack of baseball bats in vacant lots and school yards. Little League season is now underway in the United States. Girls and boys who play on Little League teams wear uniforms and are trained by coaches who know the game well.

Three-year-old horses race in the Kentucky derby on the first Saturday of May. The derby is one of the most popular sporting events in the United States, and millions of people watch it on television.

May is not a happy time for everyone. Some people are allergic to pollen from plants such as ragweed or timothy grass. Because plants of all kinds are flowering, May can be a month of sneezing, itchy eyes, and runny noses.

There are many superstitions about May. Throughout Europe, people once believed that a woman who bathed in fresh dew collected on the first of May would stay young and beautiful. In England and Scotland, some people believe that May is an unlucky month for marriages. An old saying warns: "Marry in May and you'll rue the day."

The May Birthstone

The birthstone for May is the emerald, a precious gem that comes in all shades of green. Emeralds have been worn for thousands of years, often by royalty. They were worn in Babylon, and they have been found on ancient Egyptian mummies. The Crown of the Andes, a jeweled crown said to have been worn by the last Inca ruler of Peru, was decorated with 453 emeralds.

The May Flower

If you were born in May, your special flower is the lily of the valley. In Ireland, lilies of the valley were once called fairy ladders because people believed that fairies climbed up and down the stalks of these plants by using the blossoms as rungs.

Taurus

The May Zodiac

Taurus, the bull, is the astrological sign for people with birthdays from April 20 to May 20. People born under Taurus are said to be stubborn, somewhat shy, and strong and healthy like the bull. A Taurus is also thought to be musical, artistic, and a hard worker.

The sign for people born from May 21 to June 21 is Gemini, the twins. Those born under Gemini are thought to be bright, interesting, and great company. They like to do three or four things at once. They enjoy learning foreign languages and working with their hands. It is also said that a Gemini is often late to appointments.

Gemini

the Pleiades

The Calendar

May is the fifth month of the year and has thirty-one days. There are several stories about the origin of the name of this month. It may have been named for Maia, the Roman goddess of spring and growth. The Romans held ceremonies in Maia's honor on May 1 and again on May 15.

Maia was also the name of a Greek goddess. In Greek mythology, the gods transformed Maia and her sisters into seven stars called the Pleiades. Although this story is a myth, the Pleiades is a real constellation. The rising of the Pleiades in the morning sky marks the end of spring and the beginning of summer.

Sun, Sky, and Weather

By May, most of the harshness of winter has passed. The sky is bright, and warm sunshine filters through the new leaves on the trees. Nevertheless, a breath of winter still lurks in the shadows of a May morning.

Beaches in May are often chilly, and the weather in the mountains is uncertain. But in the desert, the heat rises in late spring. At noon, the sun blazes down, and a dry wind blows sand across the mesas.

On the prairie, May weather can be icy cold, extremely hot, or anything in between. On May 7, 1989, the temperature in Manhattan, Kansas rose from a freezing thirty degrees to a balmy high of eighty-eight degrees.

May's full moon has been called the full flower moon by some Native American peoples of the Northeast. The Anglo-Saxons, who settled in Britain in the fifth and sixth centuries, called May *Thrimilce*, which means "three times milking." This is because cows feasting on the rich, green grass can be milked three times a day in May.

Animals in May

Insects hatch in the woods. Baby spiders spin silk threads and wait for breezes to carry them to new homes. Mosquitoes flit over marshes and along riverbanks. Only the female mosquitoes feed on blood from animals or people. The blood helps them produce their eggs.

Under the water, tadpoles feed on tiny plants called algae. They hide under rocks if a shadow from a larger animal passes overhead.

Hungry birds feast on the newly hatched insects. Thrushes and mockingbirds sing to attract mates and to announce their claim to a territory. Male birds of some species, such as the robin and the oriole, wear brightly colored feathers to attract females. Female birds often have brown and drab feathers to help them keep hidden while they sit on their eggs.

In the mountains, hoary marmots are also looking for mates. Marmots are playful animals, always ready for a game of tag. If a marmot spots danger, it whistles to warn its neighbors.

Desert animals must find ways to cope with the midday heat in May. Honeybees become their own air conditioners. First, the bees gather drops of water at a desert pool. After returning to the hive, each bee holds a drop between its chin and proboscis, or snout, and beats its wings rapidly. When many bees work together, the hive stays cooler.

Horned toads sit on rocks to warm themselves at daybreak. Newly hatched Gambel's quail look for water. Many quail chicks will become meals for coyotes or hawks, but some will survive to become adults.

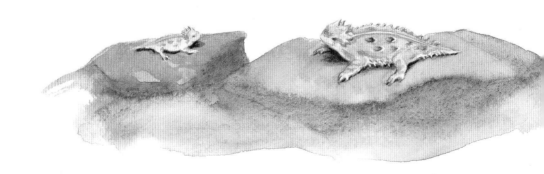

In the city, a pair of male robins races across the grass in the park. Each is daring the other to step over the imaginary line that marks the boundary of his territory.

On the prairie, the bison shed their winter coats. The hair of the bison, which is full of seeds and burs, falls off in patches until the animals look bare. Some of the seeds will fall in the dirt and start to grow. Birds and mice will use the hair to line their nests.

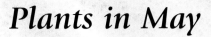

Plants in May

Pink-and-white blossoms appear on the branches of cherry and plum trees. Apple, pear, peach, and dogwood trees are covered with white and pastel-colored flowers. Oaks, hickories, and walnuts are also in bloom. Flecks of pollen from these trees coat ponds and lawns.

Lilacs bloom in most parts of North America. Buttercups, jack-in-the-pulpits, wild geraniums, and wild columbines can be found in the Northeast.

In May, paloverdes begin to flower in the desert. After a wet winter, the trees are completely covered with soft yellow blossoms.

On the prairie, the hilltops are splashed with Indian paintbrush and groundplum. Along the creeks, marsh marigolds and yellow star grass have appeared.

The new leaves on trees are busy turning sunlight into food. They do this by capturing the energy from sunlight and converting it to chemical energy by a process called photosynthesis. The plants use the energy from sunlight to make a simple sugar. When people and animals eat plants, they, too, can make use of this stored energy. In fact, all our food comes, in one way or another, from plants and from photosynthesis.

In the city, people plant bright spring flowers in flower boxes in front of stores and underneath windows. Dahlias, gladiolas, and lilies add color to May gardens.

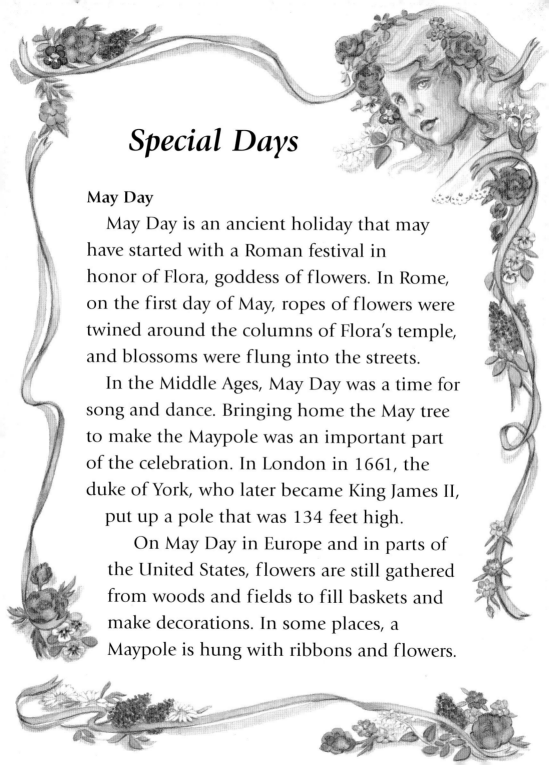

Special Days

May Day

May Day is an ancient holiday that may have started with a Roman festival in honor of Flora, goddess of flowers. In Rome, on the first day of May, ropes of flowers were twined around the columns of Flora's temple, and blossoms were flung into the streets.

In the Middle Ages, May Day was a time for song and dance. Bringing home the May tree to make the Maypole was an important part of the celebration. In London in 1661, the duke of York, who later became King James II, put up a pole that was 134 feet high.

On May Day in Europe and in parts of the United States, flowers are still gathered from woods and fields to fill baskets and make decorations. In some places, a Maypole is hung with ribbons and flowers.

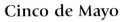

Cinco de Mayo

The fifth of May, called Cinco de Mayo in Spanish, is a special day for Mexicans and Mexican Americans. On May 5, 1862, in Puebla, Mexico, the Mexican army drove back the more powerful French forces of Napoleon III. The French army had hoped to capture Mexico City and gain control of the entire country.

In the United States, Mexican Americans celebrate Cinco de Mayo with fiestas, mariachi bands, and delicious Mexican food. People display the Mexican flag, and piñatas are hit with sticks until they break, scattering candy for everyone.

Mother's Day

Mother's Day is a time for people to show love, respect, and appreciation for their mothers, or for someone who has acted as a mother to them. In 1908, a woman named Anna Jarvis asked her mother's church in Grafton, West Virginia, to observe Mother's Day on the second Sunday in May. In 1914, President Woodrow Wilson set aside that day for people in the United States to celebrate Mother's Day as a national holiday.

Memorial Day

The Civil War was the only war ever fought by Americans against other Americans. After the war ended, some people wanted to honor all those on both sides who had died. In Columbus, Mississippi, in 1866, four women decorated the graves of both the Confederate and the Union soldiers who were buried in Friendship Cemetery. Newspapers throughout the country wrote about this act of forgiveness.

In Waterloo, New York, at about the same time, a druggist named Henry C. Welles organized a parade of veterans and townspeople. The people marched to the local cemetery and decorated all of the soldiers' graves with flags and flowers. They called this day Decoration Day.

In 1868, the United States government adopted Decoration Day as a national holiday. Later the name was changed to Memorial Day. Now, all American soldiers who gave their lives for their country are honored in ceremonies on Memorial Day.

Famous May Events

On May 10, 1869, the tracks of the Union Pacific Railroad were joined to those of the Central Pacific Railroad at Promontory, Utah. For the first time, railroad tracks linked the United States from the Atlantic Ocean to the Pacific. A golden spike, worth about four hundred dollars, was driven into a railroad tie to celebrate the event. The spike was removed after the ceremony and is now in the Art and History Museum at Stanford University in California.

On May 18, 1910, Halley's comet passed between the earth and the sun. A few astronomers had predicted that poisonous gas from the comet's tail would kill all life on the planet. Although other astronomers disagreed, fear spread throughout the world. At its closest approach, the comet was spectacular, and the tail proved entirely harmless.

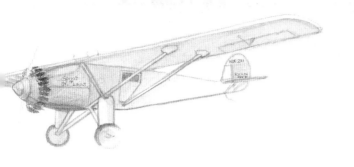

On May 21, 1927, Captain Charles Lindbergh, a 25-year-old aviator, became the first person to fly nonstop from New York City to Paris, France. When he arrived in France in his plane, *Spirit of St. Louis*, he was awarded a twenty-five-thousand-dollar prize for his feat and was nicknamed Lucky Lindy. He instantly became a world hero.

On May 18, 1980, Mount St. Helens erupted in southern Washington. The first nine-hour blast flattened forests and scattered trees. Rocks as big as cars were hurled through the air. A dark column of ash rose miles into the sky and blew eastward. In Yakima, Washington, the sky was so dark that streetlights went on at noon.

Birthdays

Many famous people were born in May.

Benjamin Spock

May 2, 1903

Noted pediatrician and author of *Baby and Child.*

Harry S. Truman

May 8, 1884

Thirty-third president of the United States who expanded America's role in foreign affairs.

Florence Nightingale

May 12, 1820

Founder of trained nursing as a profession for women.

Joe Louis

May 13, 1914

Longest-reigning heavyweight boxing champion of the world, nicknamed the Brown Bomber.

Malcolm X

May 19, 1925

Spokesperson for the
Nation of Islam and
founder of the
Organization of Afro-
American Unity.

Sir Arthur Conan Doyle

May 22, 1859

English doctor and
detective-story writer who
created Sherlock Holmes.

Margaret Fuller

May 23, 1810

Journalist and author
of an important early
book on feminism,
*Woman in the
Nineteenth Century.*

Rachel Carson

May 27, 1907

American scientist
and leading figure in
the environmental
movement.

John F. Kennedy

May 29, 1917

Thirty-fifth president of
the United States, who
launched the Peace Corps.

Walt Whitman

May 31, 1819

American poet and
author of *Leaves of Grass.*

A May Story

In the days when Pony Express riders delivered the mail, one of the most daring riders was Bob Haslam, nicknamed Pony Bob. Pony Bob always rode half-wild mustangs that could withstand the heat and hardship of the desert trail.

Pony Bob's regular route ran through western Nevada. One day in May, 1860, Pony Bob rode into the Bucklands station and delivered the mailbag to the next rider as usual. But Paiute Indians had attacked some of the other riders, and the relief man refused to take the bag. The station master turned to Bob and said, "I'll give you fifty dollars if you make the ride."

Bob accepted the offer. He rode to the Smith's Creek station, stopping briefly at the Sand Springs and Cold Springs stations along the way. It was a lonely, dangerous journey of 190 miles.

When he reached his destination, Pony Bob rested for a few hours and then began to retrace his route. On his way back, Bob discovered to his horror that the Cold Springs station had been attacked, the station master had been killed, and all the horses had been stolen.

Bob was wary, and he prepared himself for an attack. He watched the ears of his pony for any sign of danger. The night was still, and the howling of wolves and coyotes sent chills through his body. Somehow he arrived at Bucklands without mishap.

When the Bucklands station master heard Bob's story, he offered Bob another fifty dollars to carry the mail once more, this time to the Fridays station across the Sierra Nevada. After a short nap, Bob was on his way.

When Bob reached the last station, he had ridden a total of 380 miles in seventy-eight hours with only eleven hours rest. No other rider in the history of the Pony Express ever matched this record.

AUTHOR'S NOTE

This book gives an overview of the month of May in North America. But nature does not follow a strict schedule. The mating and migration of animals, the blooming of plants, and other natural events vary from year to year, or occur earlier or later in different places.

The zodiac sections of this book are included just for fun as part of the folklore of the month and should not be taken as accurate descriptions of any real people.

The story about Pony Bob Haslam was adapted from a variety of sources, including *A Thrilling and Truthful History of the Pony Express: or Blazing the Westward Way and Other Sketches and Incidents of Those Stirring Times*, by William Lightfoot Visscher. (Chicago: Charles T. Powner Co., 1946.)

Text copyright © 2002 by Ellen Jackson
Illustrations copyright © 2002 by Kay Life
All rights reserved, including the right of
  reproduction in whole or in part in any form.

Published by Charlesbridge Publishing
85 Main Street, Watertown, MA 02472
(617) 926-0329
www.charlesbridge.com

Illustrations done in watercolor on Fabriano
  hot-press paper
Display type and text type set in Giovanni
Color separations made by Sung In Printing,
  South Korea
Printed and bound by Sung In Printing,
  South Korea
Production supervision by Brian G. Walker
Designed by Diane M. Earley

Library of Congress
Cataloging-in-Publication Data

Jackson, Ellen B., 1943-
  May/Ellen Jackson; illustrated by Kay Life.
    p. cm.—(It happens in the month of)
  ISBN 0-88106-918-3 (hardcover)
  1. May (Month)—Folklore. 2. May
  (Month)—Juvenile literature. [1. May
  (Month)] I. Life, Kay, ill. II. Title.

  GR930.J339   2002
  398'.33—dc21   2001028268

Printed in South Korea
10 9 8 7 6 5 4 3 2 1